# LEAVE No Trace

*Minimum Impact Outdoor Recreation*

## THE OFFICIAL MANUAL OF AMERICAN HIKING SOCIETY

Will Harmon

D1023986

FALCON®

HELENA, MONTANA

American Hiking Society

# A FALCON GUIDE ®

Copyright © 1997 by Falcon® Publishing, Inc., Helena, Montana.
Printed in Canada.

3  4  5  6  7  8  10  TP  05  04  03  02  01  00

Falcon and FalconGuide are registered trademarks of Falcon® Publishing, Inc.

All rights reserved, including the right to reproduce any part of this book
in any form, except brief quotations for reviews, without written
permission of the publisher.

Editing, design, typesetting and other pre-press work by Falcon®
Publishing, Inc.

Illustrations by Lisa Harvey.


Library of Congress Cataloging-in-Publication Data
Harmon, Will.
    Leave no trace : minimum impact outdoor recreation / Will Harmon.
      p.  cm.
    Includes bibliographical references (p. 118)
    ISBN 1-56044-581-5 (pbk.)
    1. Low-impact camping.  2. Camping—Environmental aspects.
  3. Outdoor recreation—Environmental aspects.  4. Hiking—
Environmental aspects.  I. Title.
GV198.93.H37   1997
796.54—dc21                         97-15974
                                          CIP

**CAUTION**

Outdoor recreation activities are by their very nature potentially hazardous.
All participants in such activities must assume the responsibility for their
own actions and safety. The information contained in this guidebook cannot
replace sound judgment and good decision-making skills, which help reduce
risk exposure involved in such activities.

    Learn as much as possible about the outdoor recreation activities you
participate in, prepare for the unexpected, and be safe and cautious. The
reward will be a safer and more enjoyable experience.

# Acknowledgments

For showing the way, thanks to David Cole and the staff at the USDA Forest Service Aldo Leopold Wilderness Institute. Appreciation also goes to the members of and contributors to the Master Network at the National Leave No Trace Program.

# Contents

# Why Is It Important to Leave No Trace?

Most of us follow familiar routines when we travel or camp in the backcountry. We lace up a pair of comfortable old boots, glance at a map, and head for the hills. At camp, we sweep out a tent site, set up a kitchen, and kindle a fire as the stars come out. For many of us, these habits are what camping is all about—they define our backcountry experience.

The leave-no-trace ethic asks us to change our definition, at least slightly. To consider switching to boots with a low-profile sole, to refrain from "preparing" a site before camping there, perhaps even to forego the evening campfire.

"But this is my camping trip," you say. "Why should I bother changing the way I've always done things?"

The answer is simple: if we don't learn to leave no trace, the backcountry will be loved to death. The ground will become bare and hard under a thunder of footfalls, wildlife will flee, and other people will grumble about the eroded trails, noise, litter, and the scars on the land.

The fact is land owners and managers are faced with more and more people recreating on a shrinking supply of natural lands. To protect the land, its wildlife, and the quality of everyone's recreational experience, land managers are often forced to impose regulations or restrict access. They may limit the number of people who can use a site at any one time. Or they may prohibit certain types of use.

A good example of the problem (and the regulatory solution) is found at Lake Solitude in Grand Teton National Park. At 9,035 feet above sea level and 10 miles from the end of the road, Lake Solitude was aptly named. For years relatively few people made the arduous climb to its shores. Those who did were rewarded with unspoiled solitude amid spectacular alpine scenery. Some of us remember watching from sleeping bags at the water's edge as sunrise gilded the face of the Grand Teton.

But the 1960s saw an unprecedented explosion in backcountry recreation. In less than a decade the numbers of people visiting Lake Solitude and places like it went from hundreds or thousands in a single year to tens of thousands. The lake no longer lived up to its name. Fragile alpine plants were trampled till they could not grow back. Rocks and boulders bore scars from countless campfires and the ground was picked clean of downed wood. People—and signs of their presence—had become the dominant feature of Lake Solitude.

Park managers are mandated to protect the land and preserve the public's opportunity for a wilderness experience. They responded to the overall increase in backcountry use and resultant damage by requiring permits for overnight stays. They also restricted camping to certain zones, mostly

below timberline. Eventually, open fires were also prohibited in the Teton backcountry. Today a no-camping buffer
surrounds Lake Solitude, limiting use to day visits from the
trailhead or from basecamps elsewhere along the trail. The
area is recovering, albeit slowly, thanks to these management
decisions.

Other wild places have also been damaged or are still at
risk. The backcountry has become a crowded place. But the
leave-no-trace ethic provides an alternative to regulations.
Land managers know that many people can pass through a
place without damaging it if they are careful. Learning to
leave no trace is mostly a matter of understanding how to
travel and camp in the backcountry with a reasonable amount
of care.

### The Problem . . .

When people venture into the backcountry, they leave a mark
on their surroundings—it can't be helped. Even the most
skilled and careful hiker will leave footprints, a urine sam-
ple, grass flattened beneath a tent. In fragile environments
or where use is heavy, the damage can be much more severe—trails too eroded to walk on, water polluted with
human waste, and whole galaxies of fire rings clustered
around popular campsites.

Wildlife and recreationists can also suffer adverse af-
fects. Animals are stressed when people come too close. Some
animals—such as bears—grow accustomed to people or learn
to associate humans with food from improper disposal of

garbage. This leads to dangerous encounters, and the area is closed to further use or the animals are killed. Other recreationists seeking solitude may be disturbed by finding litter or hearing the noise of nearby campers.

As we look at ways to soften our presence in the backcountry, it helps to remember the three types of adverse effects.

**Physical**—changes to the landscape and soil
**Biological**—disturbance of wildlife and plants
**Social**—intrusion on other people

### *. . . and the Cure*

To prevent or reduce these adverse effects, we need to know what kinds of backcountry behavior are appropriate and what kinds are harmful—in short, what's right and what's wrong. In his book, *A Sand County Almanac*, Aldo Leopold wrote, "A thing is right when it tends to preserve the integrity, stability, and beauty of the biotic community. It is wrong when it tends otherwise."

That's a good start, particularly if we remember that humans are very much a part of that biotic community. To a large degree, learning to leave no trace is about preserving our own integrity, stability, and beauty, as individuals and as a society.

But we need to add a corollary to Leopold's ethic: "In the field, the choice between right and wrong is not always clear."

### *Remember to Have Fun*

Remember why we are out there. We want to experience nature and have fun playing in paradise without doing damage to it.

# Seven Principles*
# of Leave-No-Trace
# Behavior

When choices are difficult, we need some guidelines, a simple code of behavior to preserve the land, our freedoms, and our other recreational opportunities. The following seven principles are the official principles of Leave No Trace, Inc., and are copyrighted by LNT, Inc. and the National Outdoor Leadership School. Reprinted here with permission.

### 1. PLAN AHEAD AND PREPARE

- Know the regulations and special concerns for the area you will visit.
- Prepare for extreme weather, hazards, and emergencies.
- Schedule your trip to avoid times of high use.
- Visit in small groups. Split larger parties into groups of 4–6.
- Repackage food to minimize waste.
- Use a map and compass to eliminate the use of marking paint, rock cairns or flagging.

## 2. TRAVEL AND CAMP ON DURABLE SURFACES

- Durable surfaces include established trails and campsites, rock, gravel, dry grasses or snow.
- Protect riparian areas by camping at least 200 feet from lakes and streams.
- Good campsites are found, not made. Altering a site is not necessary. In popular areas
- Concentrate use on existing trails and campsites.
- Walk single file in the middle of the trail, even when wet or muddy.
- Keep campsites small. Focus activity in areas where vegetation is absent. In pristine areas
- Disperse use to prevent the creation of campsites and trails.
- Avoid places where impacts are just beginning.

## 3. DISPOSE OF WASTE PROPERLY

- Pack it in, pack it out. Inspect your campsite and rest areas for trash or spilled foods. Pack out all trash, leftover food, and litter.
- Deposit solid human waste in catholes dug 6 to 8 inches deep at least 200 feet from water, camp, and trails. Cover and disguise the cathole when finished.
- Pack out toilet paper and hygiene products.

- To wash yourself or your dishes, carry water 200 feet away from streams or lakes and use small amounts of biodegradable soap. Scatter strained dishwater.

## 4. LEAVE WHAT YOU FIND

- Preserve the past: examine, but do not touch, cultural or historic structures and artifacts.
- Leave rocks, plants and other natural objects as you find them.
- Avoid introducing or transporting non-native species.
- Do not build structures, furniture, or dig trenches.

## 5. MINIMIZE CAMPFIRE IMPACTS

- Campfires can cause lasting impacts to the backcountry. Use a lightweight stove for cooking and enjoy a candle lantern for light.
- Where fires are permitted, use established fire rings, fire pans, or mound fires.
- Keep fires small. Only use sticks from the ground that can be broken by hand.
- Burn all wood and coals to ash, put out campfires completely, then scatter cool ashes.

## 6. RESPECT WILDLIFE

- Observe wildlife from a distance. Do not follow or approach them.
- Never feed animals. Feeding wildlife damages their health, alters natural behaviors, and exposes them to predators and other dangers.
- Protect wildlife and your food by storing rations and trash securely.
- Control pets at all times, or leave them at home.
- Avoid wildlife during sensitive times: mating, nesting, raising young, or winter.

## 7. BE CONSIDERATE OF OTHER VISITORS

- Respect other visitors and protect the quality of their experience.
- Be courteous. Yield to other users on the trail.
- Step to the downhill side of the trail when encountering pack stock.
- Take breaks and camp away from trails and other visitors.
- Let nature's sounds prevail. Avoid loud voices and noises.

### *In Popular Places, Concentrate Use*

The main objective in popular places is to confine activities to areas already damaged by previous use. This preserves adjacent unspoiled areas. And the bare, compacted soil of popular sites is often hardened to use—additional use is unlikely to damage it any further.

- Stay on established trails.
- Use existing campsites well away from water, main trails, and other campers.
- Use existing fire rings, but build fires only if downed wood is abundant.
- Pack out all human waste or deposit it in cat holes at least 200 feet from surface water and in spots unlikely to be used by others.
- Leave a clean camp so others will also use it and not be tempted to create a new site.

### *In Pristine Places, Disperse Use*

The main objective in pristine places is to minimize trampling and other damage by spreading use over a wide area or by seeking out durable surfaces. This prevents others from following in your footsteps, and so reduces the likelihood of repeated use of any one travel route or campsite.

- Keep group size small; two to six people is best, no more than ten (use extra care to minimize damage when traveling with larger groups).

- When traveling off-trail, spread out so that no one follows in another's footsteps. Or follow routes on durable surfaces such as sand, gravel, exposed bedrock, or snow. Avoid steep slopes.
- Camp on durable surfaces or in areas with trample-resistant plants such as in dry meadows.
- Move camp frequently, once a day if possible. Avoid walking repeatedly over the same terrain.
- Refrain from building fires. If one is necessary, use a fire pan or build a mound fire (see pages 42–43).
- Pack out all human waste whenever possible. If this is impossible, use a cat hole (see pages 47–49).
- Leave no trace of your stay when breaking camp. Fluff up flattened grass, cover bare areas with leaves and twigs, and pick up all litter.

### *Avoid Places that are Lightly Worn or Just Beginning to Show Signs of Use*

The main objectives in places just beginning to show wear are to avoid adding to the damage already done and to allow the site to recover.

- Stay off unofficial trails or paths that are indistinct or partly vegetated.
- Seek out well-worn campsites or previously unused sites on durable surfaces.

- To discourage others from using lightly worn campsites, dismantle any fire rings, wood piles, or other structures, and camouflage the area as you would a pristine campsite.

---

**NOTE:** One final guideline, which overrides all the others: where an agency or landowner has established rules and regulations, know and obey them. Rules are there to preserve the land and protect you and your fellow recreationists. Heeding them ensures everyone an opportunity to have fun in the great outdoors.

---

# Leave-No-Trace Techniques

This book presents the nuts and bolts of the leave-no-trace approach to outdoor travel and camping. The behaviors and skills suggested here are based on common sense as well as field research. They require no real sacrifice of comfort or convenience, but neither are they watered-down versions of some higher code of ethics. Instead, we offer a range of options whenever possible to help you cope with a myriad of natural environments, special situations, and unique or unexpected challenges.

When learning to leave no trace, it's important to realize that different techniques work for different environments and circumstances. The right boots for scaling an ice-clad mountain would wreak havoc on a water-logged meadow. A good tent site in a heavily visited area is far different than a good tent site in pristine wilderness.

In short, the most important trait of a no-trace traveler is the ability to adapt to one's surroundings. And this is more a matter of attitude than skill or special knowledge. It's a frame of mind grounded in awareness and respect for the land, its inhabitants, and other visitors. If you bring that respect with you, the following techniques practically work by themselves.

## TRIP PLANNING

Planning a backcountry trip is an enjoyable process, a heightening of anticipation before the day of departure. We pore over maps, air out the tent, and stomp around the house in old, worn-out hiking boots "to break them in." These rituals, as fun as they are, are also fundamental to the success of any outing, whether you measure success on a scale of fun, adventure, safety, or leaving no trace—or all of the above. To get the most out of any trip, follow the credo: "Plan, prepare, prevent."

### *Plan Ahead*

The first step on most backcountry journeys is deciding where and when to go. The key to good planning lies in knowing what to expect when you get there. The more you know about a place, the better you'll be able to leave no trace of your visit. Before you hit the trail, learn about the area's weather, wildlife, and recreational use patterns. Read guidebooks and magazine articles, look at maps, and call or write ahead for local information. Then consider the following factors:

- Most backcountry use occurs in the summer and fall. Trails and campsites are busiest on weekends and holidays. Also, 80 percent of wildland recreational use is concentrated on just 20 percent of the land. Think about your goals for each outing and choose an area and time well-suited to those goals. When solitude is important, plan to go during mid-week or during a less popular season, and seek out a less heavily used area. When you're focused more on a specific activity than on a particular place, consider visiting an area that is less sensitive to use. To hone your racing skills on a mountain bike, for example, avoid busy or muddy trails in favor of little-used trails or hardpacked dirt roads.

- Avoid backcountry travel when trails and soils are likely to be wet. Factor in spring snowmelt, which varies greatly by elevation, latitude, and rainy seasons.

- Avoid travel through important wildlife habitat (such as nesting or calving grounds) during sensitive seasons. Learn about the ecology of an area before you visit to avoid causing inadvertent harm.

- Choose places and trails specifically suited to your planned type of use. Try to avoid places and times where conflicts between different types of backcountry users may arise.

### *Prepare Well*

With the proper equipment, appropriate clothing and shelter, and adequate food, you can relax and enjoy the trip. Well-prepared travelers also do less harm to the land. For example, if wet weather is unavoidable, waterproof your boots so you won't be tempted to step off-trail when the going gets muddy. Also, carry a good tent, rain gear, and extra clothes to avert the need for an emergency campfire.

- To be as inconspicuous as possible, choose muted, earth-tone colors for your clothes, tent, and backpack (but wear blaze orange for safety during hunting season).

- Draw up a checklist of essential items for backcountry travel and refer to it before packing for each trip. Leaving no trace doesn't require any special tools, but two items do come in handy: a small trowel for digging cat holes and a few plastic bags for packing out garbage. If you repack all your food in plastic bags, you can use these for garbage as the food is eaten.

- Make sure your equipment is in good working condition and all the parts are in place before you leave. For extended trips, carry an extra stove or spare parts to avoid cooking over a fire out of necessity.

- For longer trips, buy a water filter and learn how to use and clean it.

- Calculate and pre-pack the amount of food needed for each person. This keeps leftovers—an unpleasant item to pack out—to a minimum. When traveling with pack-stock, determine how much feed to carry for each animal.

### Prevent Problems before They Occur

It's much easier to prevent damage to the land and its inhabitants than it is to fix the problem after the fact. Here's a handful of easy precautions everyone should take before setting out:

- Call or write to the land manager. Ask about any special regulations, permits, or fees. Find out if there are recommended no-trace measures unique to that area.
- Check the weather forecast. Pack or change travel plans accordingly.
- Do a quick inventory for unneeded weight. Some items are best left at home: bottled or canned food, aluminum foil, axes and saws, guns (when not hunting), radios and tape or CD players, wire, nails, and pets.

## WALKING SOFTLY

The most widespread type of damage caused by recreational use is trampling. In 1977 Dr. William Harlow scraped up the soil left standing on the trail in a single print from a traditional lug-soled boot. He dried it in the sun and weighed it—a total of slightly more than one ounce. Assuming an average stride of 2.5 feet, Dr. Harlow calculated that a single hiker walking 1 mile would leave about 120 pounds of topsoil vulnerable to erosion.

Dr. Harlow's experiment may not represent typical trail conditions, but it does provide a dramatic explanation for the trenches that pass for trails in some of our heavily used recreation areas.

A shallower tread pattern on the sole won't clog with mud and does far less damage to soil and plants. For general, all-terrain hiking try a pair of trail running shoes or cross-training athletic shoes. They're lightweight, which lessens fatigue, and they dry out more quickly than full-grain leather boots. If you need more support, try a pair of light or ultra-light hiking boots. Most models feature low-profile soles.

| **FEATURES OF A NO-TRACE HIKING BOOT** |
| --- |
| A comfortable fit right out of the box. |
| Waterproof or water-repellent uppers. |
| A low-profile outer sole of "tacky" rubber for traction. |
| Stiff, padded ankle support and good arch support. |

### *Slip into Something More Comfortable*

In camp, where foot traffic is heaviest, take off your sweaty boots and slip on a pair of camp shoes. The ideal camp shoe is lightweight and soft-soled. Running shoes, sport sandals, or canvas boat shoes work well. They pack easily and can double as wading shoes for stream crossings.

## EXOTIC PLANTS

When botanists talk of exotics they mean non-native species, plants that are introduced to an area. Almost by definition, most exotics are champion hitchhikers. Burrs affix to clothes or hair, seeds sift into pockets or baggage, and whole plants are uprooted and tangled onto car axles or mufflers.

Exotics cause problems because they can overrun the natural botanic community. Many exotics are also harmful to wildlife and livestock. Some plants are less nutritious than native forage, while others are actually toxic to browsing animals. A few, like spotted knapweed, can strangle an animal's intestines.

Land owners and managers spend millions of dollars each year trying to curb the spread of such noxious weeds. They often respond to the threat of a weed invasion by restricting or closing recreational access. But this can be prevented if recreationists learn to inspect for exotics on their vehicles, clothes, and packstock. Remember: a single seed can infest a whole new region.

- Before leaving home, check your vehicle for hitchhiking weeds. Inspect your clothing for burrs and seeds. Look in pants cuffs, pockets, on socks and shoelaces.
- Carefully inspect packstock—especially tails, manes, and legs—for burrs and seeds before loading animals into trailers. Feed for packstock should be certified weed-and-seed free.

- Mountain bicycles and all-terrain vehicles can also snag weeds. Keep an eye on spokes, chain rings, and sprockets for stowaways.

- Inspect boat trailers, hulls, engines, propellers, paddles, and oars for clinging weeds and other aquatic life (such as zebra mussels) when pulling out of the water. Do not transport water, live bait, or fish from one source to another.

- When eating fruits, vegetables, nuts in their shells, or seeds with husks (e.g., sunflower seeds), stash the pits, cores, rinds, peels, shells, husks, and other scraps in a plastic bag. Pack out all such garbage.

### ROUTE SELECTION

Most backcountry travelers rarely stray far off established trails, and from a no-trace perspective that's good. Trails tend to channel people through well-used corridors, leaving large chunks of real estate relatively untouched. In some wilderness areas as much as 80 percent of backcountry use is concentrated on just 20 percent of the area's available trails. In other words, most people not only stick to established trails, but they favor the most well-traveled routes.

### *In Popular Places*

Good route selection means trying to reduce damage to existing trails, particularly where erosion and heavy use is already evident.

- Avoid travel when trails are saturated with water. Check the weather forecast.
- Stay on the trail. Do not short cut switchbacks when climbing or descending a slope. Don't detour around muddy stretches.
- Walk single file.
- If the trail becomes too faint to follow, stop and scan ahead for the most trample-resistant route for the direction you wish to go.
- On busy trails, move well off-trail during rest stops. Use existing side trails and choose a durable rest site—a rock outcrop, gravel stream bank, sandy area, or dry meadow.
- Ask for permission before crossing private property. Leave all gates as you found them.

### *In Pristine Places*

Where there are no trails, cross-country travel requires extra precaution and a willingness to tread lightly.

- Select a route that follows durable surfaces. Look for ribbons of bedrock, slickrock, sand, gravel, and snow pack. Gravel or sand riverbanks and lake shores offer good routes. Try to stay below the high-water line.

- Stay off game trails unless cross-country travel would do more damage to plants and soil.

- Where no durable surfaces are available, have the group spread out so no one follows in another's footsteps.

- Keep party size small—fewer than 10 people.

- Except in emergencies, leave your route unmarked. Leave no blazes, cairns, flagging, or arrows made of sticks or drawn in the dirt.

## CULTURAL ARTIFACTS

Backcountry travelers occasionally stumble across stone te-pee rings, ancient burial grounds, prehistoric arrowheads and spear points, petroglyphs, and—particularly in the desert canyons of the Southwest—pottery shards and ruins of re-markable stone houses and villages. These artifacts are as much a part of the landscape as wildflowers or birdsong.

- Leave all artifacts and structures undisturbed. Hand oils can discolor stone and other surfaces, so do not touch pottery, rock paintings, or carvings. Collecting such ar-tifacts (and fossils) is prohibited on all federal and most state lands.

- Camp well away from historic or cultural sites, and walk softly when passing through. If you happen upon a site that you suspect is a new find, mark it on your map and jot down detailed directions for how to find it again. Report all such finds to the local office of the managing agency or to the archaeology department of a nearby university.

### *Native Peoples*

A few places remain where traditional—sometimes ancient—ways of life still prevail. Native peoples across the Arctic, in the Southwest, and in other regions still pursue subsistence hunting, fishing, trapping, and wild plant harvesting as a respected and preferred way of life.

As a visitor, be courteous and show respect for others' beliefs, language, customs, and history. Learn about the culture before your visit, and know and obey tribal regulations.

- Ask permission before trespassing on tribal or village lands.

- Ask permission before taking photographs.

- Where subsistence lifestyles are practiced, don't harvest wild game or other food unless invited to do so.

### KEEP NOISE TO A MINIMUM

Silence is an almost tangible feature of the landscape in remote wildlands, especially to ears accustomed to ringing telephones, chattering televisions, and the hum and throb of city traffic. A recent study found daytime noise levels as low as 20 decibels in Glacier National Park and in several of Utah's canyonland parks. Dinosaur National Monument ranks as the nation's quietest place at 11 decibels (for comparison, a whisper rattles the ear at 15 to 30 decibels).

Remember the social impacts we mentioned in the preface? Noise created by other people is one of the most frequently cited complaints by backcountry travelers. Unnecessary shouting, whistling, gunfire, and other cacophony can spoil another person's sense of solitude or peace and quiet.

So go quietly in the backcountry. Leave radios, tape decks, CD players, and headphones at home. Remember that sound travels well downwind, across lakes, and in open areas. Noise may be more annoying to others at night and in the early morning.

There is one circumstance when extra noise is warranted—when traveling in bear country. Clap, sing, or make metallic noises to ward off bears. For detailed suggestions on traveling safely in bear habitat, read the book *Bear Aware* (Falcon 1996).

## CHOOSING A CAMPSITE

Most backcountry campsites were carved out of the landscape not by work crews with saws and shovels, but by sheer dint of their popularity. Anyone, it seems, can recognize a good campsite: level, well-drained ground; shelter from wind and weather; access to clean water; and, with any luck, pleasant scenery. In heavily visited areas, weary travelers add one more criterion to the list—availability.

These same traits come to play in choosing a good no-trace campsite, but from a slightly different angle. Convenience matters less than damage control. Level, well-drained ground may offer a good night's sleep, but it also requires no "engineering" (such as trenches to drain runoff away from the tent), and it is less vulnerable to erosion. Similarly, access to clean water is crucial for drinking and cooking. But put the emphasis on "clean" rather than "access." After all, what good is access if the water is polluted? The key to keeping a stream or lake free of contamination is to camp well away from it—at least 200 feet from the water's edge.

When you can't decide whether to use a site, look at the site piece by piece. (Leave plenty of time for this at the end of the day—fatigue or running out of daylight are poor reasons for choosing a campsite.)

- Has the site been used before? Heavily, moderately, lightly, or not at all?
- How trample-resistant are the soil and plants? Are durable surfaces—such as sand, gravel, or rock—available?
- Is there a potential for runoff, erosion, or water contamination?
- If you want or need a fire, is downed wood abundant?
- Ask, "When I leave this place, will there be no trace that I camped here?"

### *In Popular Places*

In places with established, well-worn sites, the main objective is to confine tents, foot traffic, and other use to areas already damaged by previous use, and to prevent additional damage.

- Where sites are designated, follow the rules.
- Look for a level, well-drained tent pad at least 200 feet from water, trails, and other campers. It may not be possible to find an existing site that meets all of these criteria (rugged terrain may limit suitable sites), but look around rather than settling on the most convenient site. Pitch your tent on a patch of bare dirt, with the door and likely traffic patterns avoiding areas where plants still have a foothold.

- Stay off lightly used or unofficial sites.
- Camp away from other campers, or position your tent to screen it from neighbors. Be quiet in camp.
- Use established paths. Avoid making new "social trails."
- Walk with extra care around seedling trees.
- Leave the site better than you found it. Pick up litter. If there is a fire ring, clean it out, leave the rocks in place, and scatter the ashes.

### *In Pristine Places*

In places that show little or no sign of previous use, the main objective is to spread use over a wide area so that no one place receives heavy traffic or disturbance. Concentrate use only on durable or trample-resistant surfaces, when available.

- Look for a level, well-drained site on sand, gravel, bedrock, or dry grass meadow.
- Leave rocks, logs, and other features in place. If moving a rock or log is unavoidable, return it to its original position when breaking camp.
- Spread out—pitch tents well apart and avoid congregating in one spot.
- Cook and eat on a durable surface 100 yards or more from tents. Minimize foot traffic between tents and the kitchen. To prevent forming a path, walk a different route for each trip between high-use areas. Watch your feet to reduce trampling.

- Look for animal tracks, scat, and evidence of feeding. Do not camp in areas frequented by wildlife.
- Minimize wear and tear on trees by not stringing up a hammock, cutting off branches, climbing, or damaging bark unnecessarily.
- Keep a clean camp so animals are not attracted by food odors or garbage.
- When breaking camp, scatter leaves, pine needles, and other natural debris over any scuffed spots. With a stick or your fingers, fluff up grass where tents flattened it. Take one last look around for litter, worn spots, or other signs of your visit. Leave no trace of your stay and you will reduce the likelihood that anyone else will be lured to camp at the same site.

### THE BACKCOUNTRY KITCHEN

Today's backcountry kitchen is highly portable—a small stove and fuel bottle, a set of nesting pots and a lid that doubles as a skillet, basic utensils, and a water bottle. Larger stoves can be carried by packstock or boaters, but the basic outfit remains the same. This self-contained kitchen bestows considerable freedom on the backcountry traveler in choosing a site for cooking, whether in popular or pristine areas.

### *In Popular Places*

Set up the kitchen around an existing fire ring or in the middle of a well-used site. Base the stove on a large rock or patch of sand. In bear habitat, cook around an existing fire ring and pitch the tent at least 200 yards distant (and upwind).

### *In Pristine Places*

Look for a durable surface such as a large rock, a patch of sand or gravel, or a beach below the high- water mark. Groups of four or more people should limit the number of cooks to reduce trampling in the kitchen area. Large groups should divide into pairs or trios and set up separate kitchens.

### *No-Trace Meals*

- Mealtime usually entails a lot of unpacking, sorting, and spreading out. Try to contain this mess within the confines of a hardened site such as a patch of sand or a large, flat rock. Some people pack a small canvas or cordura ground cloth (about 30 inches square) on which to spread their utensils and food.

- Always set the cookstove in a stable, level place, out of the wind and well away from flammables such as clothes, tents, and dry plants.

- Use only clean pots when dipping into lakes and streams for cooking or wash water. Use a water bag to reduce foot traffic to and from the water source.

- Before adding food ingredients, boil untreated water for five minutes to kill any microorganisms.

- Clean pots and pans with a plastic mesh scrubber; soap is not needed. Pick out food particles and residue and pack this out in a double plastic bag.

- Disperse wash water over the ground at least 200 yards from any likely campsite and 200 feet from any water source. Wash water can also be emptied into the established fire ring if a fire is later built there to burn off any food residue.

- Consider leaving your stove at the bottom of your pack (or at home if you're sure you won't need it to boil water for drinking or to heat a meal to ward off hypothermia) and eat only ready-to-eat food.

### CAMPFIRES

For eons a roaring fire was the center of any camp. It provided heat for warmth and cooking, light to work or read by, and a focal point for people to gather around. With the advent of lightweight, efficient cookstoves, many campers now think of campfires as a luxury or emergency tool. Land managers have also adopted this view, banning open fires in the backcountry of many national parks and wilderness areas.

By going without a fire, however, campers also forego a fire's warmth, utility, and charm. Just as one person's vice is another's virtue, there are two sides to every facet of a fire:

- A fire provides heat against night's chill, but it also anchors you to the spot. Several layers of warm, dry clothing allow you to take a moonlit stroll and still retain ample body heat. Fires are also notorious for scorching your face while your backside freezes.

- Collecting fuel and building a fire is work. Doing without a fire may provide a welcome rest at the end of a hard day on the trail.

- Cooking over an open fire adds flavor, but not all foods are enhanced by the tang of wood smoke. A cookstove is more efficient, offers better heat control, is easier to start regardless of the weather, and won't blacken your pots and pans.

- A campfire's glow is at once cheerful, useful, and reassuring. It illuminates our smiles, the lines on a map, and the shadows that would otherwise engulf camp. Admittedly, the beam from a flashlight lacks a fire's personality, but it's portable, can be aimed precisely, and turns on or off with a snap. For doing chores, a gas or battery lantern outshines any fire, and a two-ounce candle lantern provides plenty of light for cleaning dishes or reading.

- Finally, while wood smoke may be the incense of memory to some folks, the tears in their eyes are most likely due to simple irritation.

### *When Fire is Appropriate*

Despite the advantages of going fireless, nearly everyone feels that primal urge now and then. And even well-prepared, expert backcountry travelers aren't immune to emergencies, when a fire may provide life-saving warmth, hot food, or dry clothes.

The key to building a no-trace campfire is knowing when a fire is appropriate and when it is not. Here are some general guidelines:

- Know and obey local campfire regulations. Pack a stove for cooking.

- Build fires only when it is safe to do so. Do without a fire during dry or windy weather, especially if nearby groundcover and trees are dry. Remember that a single hot ember can set ablaze thousands of acres of wild country. Never leave a fire unattended.

- Build fires only where downed, dead wood is plentiful. Use only sticks that can be broken with your bare hands.

- Do without a fire in environments where plant growth is slow (such as in deserts, above timberline, and on the Arctic tundra).

- If you decide to build a campfire, remember these two objectives:

    1) leave the site as natural and pleasant looking as you found it (or better), and

    2) minimize the effects of wood gathering and of the fire itself on local soil, plants, wildlife, and other visitors.

- Gather firewood over a wide area, well away from camp. Break sticks only as needed (unused sticks can be scattered to blend in naturally).

- Keep fires small and brief. Conserve nature's supply of downed wood.

- Protect plants, soil, and rocks from the fire's heat by using a fire pan or a mound of sand or mineral soil (see illustrated instructions, pages 42–43).

- Leave existing fire rings clean and attractive for other campers.

- When building a fire in a pristine area, do not make a fire ring. Return the site to its natural condition so no one else will find and use it later.

## HOW TO BUILD A NO-TRACE FIRE

1. Gather only downed, dead wood and only as much as you will use. Sticks should be no thicker than your wrist, small enough to be broken by hand. Keep fires small and brief (use a stove for cooking, and then build a fire for drying clothes, etc.)

2. Make a six- to eight-inch mound of mineral soil in fire pan or other fire-resistant surface.

3. Or, with a trowel, dig a twelve-inch diameter pit down through the duff and top layers of organic soil to the mineral soil. Pile

the fill off to one side; if the top layer includes sod, plants, and root systems, try to keep it intact. Water this lid immediately to keep it moist and set it well away from the fire's heat.

4. Put kindling (paper, dry pine needles, or leaves) in the center of the mound or pit. Build a small tepee of twigs around the kindling; once the tepee is burning, add wood as needed.

5. Burn firewood down to a fine white ash. Use a stick to push embers and charcoal toward the center of fire to burn it down. Fan or blow on coals if needed. Soak ashes with water and stir to make sure they're cold. With your fingers, crush any remaining chunks into powder.

6. Disperse ashes by sprinkling over a wide area well away from camp and water sources.

7. Mound fire: return mound of mineral soil to the hole it came from. Sprinkle rock or ground surface with water to rinse away remaining ashes or dirt. Pit fire: backfill pit and replace sod lid.

Tamp disturbed soil lightly into place. Sprinkle water over area to replenish plant and soil moisture. Camouflage site by sweeping duff and pine needles or leaves over soil.

### *In Popular Places*

Build the fire in an existing fire ring following the guidelines above. Gather wood from a wide area away from camp. Backcountry campers can play an active role in rehabilitating popular sites by dismantling excess fire rings. Disperse the rocks over a wide area and turn blackened sides down. Leave one ring for each obvious campsite.

### *In Pristine Places*

Choose a level site with as few plants as possible. Never build a fire beneath tree branches or atop surface roots. Also, build at least 10 feet from any large rocks that could be blackened by smoke or cracked from the fire's heat. Avoid sites where rain and runoff could later drain ashes from the fire site into nearby surface water. Gently clean away plant debris that might ignite from errant sparks. Avoid any site that looks like it has been previously used.

In pristine places, there are two ways to build a no-trace fire: on a mound of sand or mineral soil (the rocky layer beneath topsoil), or in a pit. Either way, there's no need to build a rock fire ring.

Mound fires are the best choice in most circumstances because they can be built on a variety of surfaces (in a fire pan, on a large rock, or on a bare patch of ground) and they cause the least amount of disturbance to soil and plants. The fire is built on a 6-inch mound of sand or mineral soil, which insulates the surface underneath from the heat.

To build the mound, scoop up some sand or mineral soil from an inconspicuous place. Good sources are streambanks below the high-water line or holes under the root wads of recently uprooted trees. Carry the material to the fire site in a stuff sack (turned inside out to keep the inside clean). Build the mound in a fire pan if possible. An old pie tin works well, or a sheet of aluminum foil. Even a scrap of flame-retardant canvas, cut from a discarded wall tent, will do the job. Commercial fire pans are also available. On the fire pan, rock, or other surface, shape the sand or mineral soil into a 6-inch mound about 12 inches in diameter. Follow the steps in the illustrations to build a small fire on the mound.

A pit fire is appropriate when a good source of sand or mineral soil is unavailable. Use a small hand trowel to excavate the pit. DO NOT dig in dense plant cover—such upheaval usually kills plants despite all efforts to the contrary. Follow the illustrated steps to build a small fire in the pit.

## HUMAN WASTE DISPOSAL

Even under ideal conditions, human waste may take a year or more to decompose in the wild. Plop it down in a desert or atop a frozen mountain and your little monument will last even longer. Fecal pathogens also survive a year or more, even when buried in a cat hole. Factor in the more than half a billion visitor days each year on public lands in the United States alone, and you get a feel for the magnitude of the waste disposal problems faced by land managers.

How to cope with human waste? There are two basic options: pack it out, or deposit it on site, either buried in a cat hole or—in remote regions where human discovery is unlikely—scattered on the ground.

### *Packing Out Waste*

Regulations at many popular sites now require all human waste to be packed out. Boaters and packstock users should carry portable latrines—ammo cans and plastic buckets lined with plastic bags are popular options.

A newer method relies on a commercially available aluminum box with an o-ring lid that can be tightly sealed. A toilet seat replaces the lid when in use. Waste goes directly into the box, eliminating the need for plastic liner bags (which foul pumping systems and resist decomposition at landfills). At the end of the trip, the box is emptied at an RV dump station or city sewage treatment plant.

Hikers, kayakers, bikers, and others who travel light can carry a "poop tube"—a 4-inch diameter piece of pvc pipe capped at one end and threaded for a screw-on lid on the other end. To use the poop tube, scoop waste from the ground into a paper lunch bag, roll up the bag, and slide it into the tube. Screw down the lid, and the poop tube can be strapped to the outside of your pack or lashed with other gear to canoe stalwarts or bike racks. Don't put urine in the tube—that just adds weight and increases the risk of anaerobic composting, with its stronger smells.

Ask at the district office or ranger station for the best place to dispose of collected waste once you are out of the backcountry. Most national parks have a sewage treatment plant. On national forests and BLM lands, drive to the nearest town with a sewage treatment plant. Please do not put waste into outhouses unless instructed to do so. There's too big a risk of spillage, and most outhouses are drained on a regular schedule, with little room for excess waste. Finally, never put human waste into trash cans or dumpsters. This creates a serious health hazard—both at the trash can and later at the landfill—and is illegal.

### *The Cat Hole*

Contrary to popular wisdom, burying feces in a cat hole does not necessarily hasten decomposition. The reason for the cat hole is to contain the waste and any disease organisms it may hold. It keeps flies away, prevents contact with animals and other people, and protects surface water from contamination. This last concern is perhaps the most important. Today, no surface water is safe to drink untreated. This is due, in large part, to the spread of disease through improperly disposed of human waste.

- Anticipate. Keep an eye out for good sites before the urge hits. Keep a trowel and unscented toilet paper (if not using natural wipes) in a convenient pack pocket.
- Find an out-of-the-way site in stable soils at least 200 feet (about 70 paces) from surface water. Avoid places that show signs of flooding, carrying runoff, or groundwater seepage.

- Make sure the site is at least 200 feet from established campsites, trails, and other centers of human activity. Also avoid game runs and nesting or burrowing grounds.

- With a small hand trowel, dig a cat hole 6 to 8 inches deep. Keep the sod lid intact. Set it aside and pile the dirt right next to the hole.

- Once the hole is dug, slip off your knickers, use whatever posture works for you, and let the chips fall.

- Ideally, no-trace campers should rely on leaves, pine boughs, snow, or even smooth stones instead of toilet paper. These natural wipes can go right into the cat hole before covering it. Toilet paper degrades slowly—use as little as possible. It's best to pack out used toilet paper (in a double plastic bag). If you choose to burn it, use a campfire rather than lighting the paper in the cat hole. Burning toilet paper is risky at best, as one poor soul discovered after his flaming toilet paper ignited a 450-acre wildfire in Washington state in 1989. A federal judge held the man liable for $132,700 to help pay for the fire-fighting effort.

- When covering the waste, use a stick to stir in the first handful or two of soil. This puts soil microbes in direct contact with the waste and quickens decomposition. Add the remaining topsoil and the sod lid. Rake leaves and duff around to camouflage the site.

- When urinating, seek an out-of-the-way site far from water. Pee onto mineral soil or a patch of sand if possible. Urine can burn plants and its salty odor attracts animals that may paw or chew the area. Try to pee in a sunny spot so it will evaporate more quickly. Where local authorities recommend it, pee directly into large rivers to avoid urine build-up (with attendant odors) in the sand of beaches and likely campsites.

- Unless regulations dictate otherwise, do not dig group latrines; use individual cat holes.

- Clean your hands (see pages 50–51) and you're done.

### *Litter*

Another form of human waste—litter—is the number one problem cited by backcountry visitors. The no-trace response is simple: Pack it in, pack it out. Also, pick up what others left behind.

Back in civilization, think twice before unloading your cache of garbage in the first available trash can. Many outposts and small towns do not have official landfills or waste hauling services. Take garbage home with you to make sure it's disposed of properly.

## BATHING AND LAUNDRY

No one has yet devised a way to get truly clean without water, primarily because water is the universal solvent—it loosens and dissolves just about any kind of grime you mix it with. But that's also the hazard in backcountry hygiene: anything added or rinsed into water—soap, body oils, grease, or dirt—is carried back into the environment, wherever the water goes. In other words, water disperses pollutants.

Large lakes, rivers, and the oceans can withstand liberal amounts of skinny-dipping without harm to water quality. Smaller lakes, pools, and streams are more sensitive to contaminants, so think twice before you wade in. If you're wearing sunscreen, bug repellent, or a splash of fuel from the cookstove, wash it off before entering the water.

In any case, you don't need soap to come clean. Here's how:

Use a clean pot or collapsible bucket to scoop out some water from the lake or stream. Carry it at least two hundred feet from the source and find a large rock or patch of sand to stand on. Douse yourself and scrub with your hands or a clean, unadulterated washcloth. Rinse with a second dousing.

If you use a solar shower (a black plastic bag with a nozzle), remember to hang the bag over an erosion-resistant surface or move it between each use. If you must use soap, make sure it is biodegradable and use as little as possible. The surest way to avoid harming water quality is to wait and shower upon return to civilization.

Toothpaste is another form of soap—use as little as possible and keep it out of lakes and streams. Either spit tooth-paste into a plastic garbage bag or swallow it. (In higher concentrations fluoride is toxic. Use non-fluoridated tooth-paste if you make a habit of swallowing the suds.) If you spit toothpaste onto the ground, spray it over a wide area (away from surface water and likely tent sites) by pressing your tongue against your teeth as you spit.

Clothes can go weeks without a wash. On longer trips, carry a tub or heavy-duty plastic bag of water at least two hundred feet from the source. Do not add soap. Let clothes soak for at least ten minutes, then knead until the water turns dirty. Rinse and hang to dry.

A quick rinse with plain water is not enough when wash-ing hands after going to the bathroom. There are two no-trace ways to take care of this essential hygiene—pre-packaged hand wipes and waterless hand cleanser.

- Wipes are sold in grocery stores everywhere—look in the diaper aisle. Buy alcohol-based unscented wipes, which disinfect fairly well.

- Waterless hand cleanser is found on the shelves of auto parts stores. Mechanics use these gels or creams to cut the grease off their hands. Look for brands that include zinc pyrithione, an anti-microbial agent. Also make sure that water isn't required. Just massage a dab of cleanser between both hands, and wipe off the excess with a pa-per towel (that goes into your garbage bag).

# Guidelines For Different Types Of Recreation

Most of the techniques presented in Chapter 2 apply no matter what your particular brand of backcountry fun is. But some types of recreation raise special concerns when it comes to leaving no trace. This chapter offers specific ways to reduce impacts for a variety of recreational pursuits.

Traveling with packstock, mountain biking, riding motor vehicles, rock climbing, hunting, fishing, and other forms of backcountry recreation tend to be more regulated and restricted than ordinary foot travel because there is a greater potential for damage to the land and conflicts among different types of trail users. The vast majority of regulations are aimed at reducing impacts; please know and obey them at all times. In some cases they override one or more of the no-trace principles. For example, few pristine areas allow access to motor vehicles; rather than dispersing use, motorized users should avoid such areas altogether. Other, more suitable places are available for motorized recreation.

## SHARE THE TRAIL

Not only are more people heading into the backcountry to recreate, but they're finding ever more diverse ways to do it. A single trail may carry hikers, packstock, mountain bikers, pets, runners, and motor vehicles . . . sometimes all at once.

The potential for conflict can be high, but each of us can help minimize it by remembering that all of us share the same goal: to enjoy the wilderness.

- When meeting other people on the trail, yield the right-of-way even when it's not expected of you, unless it is unsafe to do so.
- When meeting packstock on the trail, step off to the downhill side and remain quiet and calm.
- Avoid conflicts and arguments. As far as is safe and reasonable, be tolerant of other people in the backcountry.
- Practice the gentle art of diplomacy. Be friendly and willing to consider the other person's point of view. Foster tolerance in others by being courteous, considerate, and quiet.
- When tolerance is stretched thin, consider moving to another area to get away from the offending party.
- Remember to plan ahead, choose a destination that's appropriate for the type of recreation you intend to engage in, and tailor your actions to suit your surroundings.

### PACKSTOCK

Horses and mules are the most common pack animals used on North American trails. Their heft, the use of steel shoes, and their penchant for grazing forage all add up to a serious risk of damage to trails and the landscape. This can be greatly reduced by following a number of simple precautions.

- Know your animals. Ideally, all pack animals should be healthy, reliable, calm, and well trained.

- Familiarize your animals with the packs, restraints, foods, and other equipment they will encounter in the backcountry. A storm on a remote, rocky ridge is no place for your packstock's first skirmish with a wildly flapping tent fly.

- Before you go on a trip, ask about local regulations or restrictions concerning pack animals.

- Carefully inspect packstock—especially tails, manes, and legs—for burrs and seeds before loading animals into trailers.

- Feed for packstock should be certified weed-and-seed free.

- Pack lightly and keep the number of packstock to a minimum. Use lightweight gear such as backpacking tents and stoves.

- Keep packstock out of campsites to reduce campsite damage, keep manure from underfoot, and curtail the number of flies in camp.

- Carry a fire pan and a portable latrine.

- Consider using the flat plate style of horseshoe if the terrain doesn't warrant heel and toe caulks.

- Yield the right-of-way whenever it's safe and sensible to do so. In many regions, the common rule is that packstrings going uphill have right-of-way in the morning; strings going downhill have it in the afternoon. Longer strings generally have the right-of-way over shorter strings, and riders without packstock should yield to packstrings.

- When watering your animals, look for an established ford or low, gentle banks with firm footing. Avoid steep banks, wet ground, and lush vegetation.

- As much as possible, avoid tying stock to trees. The rope can girdle a tree's bark, and the animal's hooves will quickly trample and pack the soil around the tree's base. If you do temporarily tie up, choose a sturdy tree at least 8 inches in diameter (about as big around as your thigh).

- For longer rest stops along the trail, find a dry meadow or other trample-resistant site and either hobble the stock or set up a quick high hitchline between two trees. Use webbed slings around the tree trunks, and attach the hitchline to these with a swivel to reduce chafing on the bark. Tie the hitchline about 7 feet above the ground so horses can walk under it; this helps minimize pawing. Keep packstock out of wet meadows.

- When choosing a campsite, look for pasture that will hold your stock without damaging the country. Dry grass meadows are best, preferably within sight of camp so you can keep an eye on your animals and put a quick stop to any damaging or dangerous behavior. Move stock frequently to minimize overgrazing.

- Portable electric fences are gaining favor as a way to corral packstock near camp. Some units are solar powered, saving the weight and hassle of batteries. Familiarize your animals with a fence before using it in the backcountry. And move it frequently to prevent overgrazing of any one spot.

### LLAMAS AND GOATS

According to the USDA Forest Service, llamas and goats make up about 5 percent of all packstock use in designated wilderness areas. Their proponents claim that these animals are lighter on the land, pointing out that a llama's track is similar to an elk's, but the footpad is softer so the hoof does not penetrate as far into the dirt, even in mud. Also, llama manure is almost indistinguishable from elk scat and attracts few, if any, flies.

- Most llama packers do not carry feed with them. Even a big llama (around 450 pounds) will eat only about 8 pounds of grass a day, 60 to 70 percent less than a horse. Nevertheless, some areas require feed to be packed in. Obey the regulations, and when traveling without feed, be considerate of wildlife foraging needs.

- Picketing and hitchlines are the two most popular ways to keep llamas in one place, and the same guidelines as for horses apply here.
- Keep goats well away from equipment and young trees to prevent damage from these omnivorous chewers.

### DOGS

- Bring your dog along only in areas where dogs are allowed.
- Keep your dog under control at all times. Keep your dog in sight when not on a leash. Don't let Rover chase deer or other wildlife, and restrain your dog when encountering packstock.
- Keep your dog quiet.
- Carry adequate dog food and a bowl. Collapsible bowls are available.
- Lead your dog well off-trail and away from water when it needs to defecate. Deposit the feces in a cat hole, or better yet, pack it out. Domestic dog feces are not a natural part of any backcountry environment and should be treated like human waste.

### MOUNTAIN BIKES

Mountain biking is one of the fastest growing backcountry sports. While cyclists revel in the freedom afforded by fat, knobby tires and go-anywhere gear ratios, other trail users are often less enthralled by these machines whizzing past.

When conflicts do arise, opponents of mountain bikes often point to trail damage and erosion caused by skidding or riding when trails are muddy. But more frequently, the real problem is unpleasant or unsafe encounters between bikers and hikers or packstock.

- The most important goal for the conscientious mountain biker is to minimize conflicts with other trail users. The easiest way to do this is common courtesy. Slow down when approaching others, and give a friendly greeting. Yield the right-of-way to all other trail users; give hikers plenty of room to pass.

- Ride single file when passing others. When meeting packstock head on, bikers should dismount and move to the downhill side of the trail. If overtaking a packtrain, speak out and ask for instructions. The horse riders may ask you to wait until they can find a wide spot in the trail, or they may request that you walk your bike past while the packtrain pauses.

- Anticipate encountering other people on the trail. Slow down for blind corners or where terrain or vegetation causes limited-sight distance. Try to ride during low-use periods; avoid busy trails.

- Ride in small groups. A large pack of bikers is more likely to disturb other people, packstock, and wildlife. And when riders bunch up, there's a greater tendency to hit the brakes hard or veer off-trail.

- Stay in control at all times, especially on descents. Slower speeds also prevent rocks from being thrown by tire treads—reason enough to hit the brakes when approaching other people.

- When resting, carry the bike off-trail so others may pass.

- Be discrete. Realize that a party of backpackers may have walked all day to reach their camping destination, though it took only three hours to cover the same ground by bike. The sudden arrival of a cyclist (likely traveling with no overnight gear) may destroy their illusion of remoteness.

- Wear a helmet. Not only will it protect your head, but land owners and managers don't get so anxious about liability when they see people taking responsibility for their own safety.

- For all-around riding, keep the tires inflated to the maximum pressure recommended on the sidewalls. This provides the most efficient contact between tread and ground, reducing soil disturbance. In deep sand, gravel, or snow, you may need to let some air out for better traction.

- Mountain bicycles can also snag weeds. Keep an eye on spokes, chain rings, and sprockets for stowaways.

- Check the bike for loose or damaged parts before each ride. If a part breaks or falls off during a ride, pack it out.

- Stay on roads and trails, and only ride on trails open to bicycles. Ask for permission before riding on private property; leave gates as you found them.

- When it is safe and reasonable to do so, ride out of the obvious and most-traveled line while still staying on the road or trail. Do not cut switchbacks.

- On dry ground, even the knobbiest bike tire does little or no damage to the soil, unless it is locked in a skid or spun in a hard push for traction. To avoid skids, control your speed and use both brakes, applying pressure gradually. On steep descents, shift your body weight behind the seat and over the rear tire to increase braking power on both wheels.

- Avoid riding in muddy conditions. If wet or muddy sections are short and infrequent, dismount and walk through them, carrying the bike.

- Ride directly over water bars (logs or rocks placed in the trail to divert runoff), or dismount and carry the bike over them.

## CANOES, KAYAKS, AND RAFTS

We are a water-loving species on a wet planet. The strong draw that rivers and lakes have on us, and the peculiar traits of water-borne recreation, call for a few special considerations among boaters of all kinds.

- The most important aspect of no-trace boating is protecting the water from contamination. Make a concerted effort to keep litter, food and other supplies, and equipment contained and in the boat.

- Lash gear securely to the boat to prevent loss in case you capsize. Lost gear is expensive litter.

- If you cache food or beverages under water (nature's refrigerator), don't use glass containers and don't build dams to form a pool. Double check the site to avoid leaving anything behind.

- Take into account times of high and low water when planning your trip. Know how different water levels will affect your route and campsite options.

- Confine camping and other activities to the beach or shore, below the high water mark or monthly high-tide line (when it is safe to do so without  serious risk of rapidly rising water). Any sign of your stay will be washed away by the next ebb and flow in water levels.

- The plants and soils in the zone just above the high-water mark can be highly sensitive to trampling and other damage. When traveling away from the beach or shore, go well inland to avoid this fragile zone.

- Build campfires only as needed and only where downed wood is abundant. Build the fire directly on the surface of the sand or gravel shore below the daily high-tide line or below the annual high-water mark. Use small pieces of wood and burn them down to ash.

- Carry a fire pan.

- Use a portable latrine—a commercially available aluminum box with an o-ring lid that can be tightly sealed. A

toilet seat replaces the lid when in use. Waste goes directly into the box, eliminating the need for plastic liner bags (which foul pumping systems and resist decomposition at landfills). At the end of the trip, the box is emptied at an RV dump station or city sewage treatment plant.

- Give wide berth to people on shore or in the water, especially anglers, swimmers, snorkelers, and divers.
- Remember that sounds carry well over open water. Keep noise to a minimum.

### CROSS-COUNTRY SKIING AND SNOWSHOEING

With a deep blanket of protective snow between themselves and the ground, cross-country skiers and snowshoers are free to roam widely with little concern for trampling or erosion. Other concerns, however, may be more serious when snow covers the ground. Wildlife is more easily stressed, and adequate waste disposal is more difficult. Couple these with ever-increasing numbers of winter recreationists, and it's apparent that a few special guidelines are in order.

- The main concern of backcountry travelers in winter should be to minimize disturbance to wildlife. For animals, winter means food is scarce, weather can be severe, and cold saps strength and energy stores.
- In popular areas, stay on established ski tracks or travel routes. Always ski in control.
- Where snow cover is thin, such as on wind-scoured ridges, or when the snowpack is melting off, use extra care in crossing open ground. Exposed soils and plants may be saturated with water or brittle from freezing, making them more vulnerable to trampling and erosion.
- Snow campers should dismantle snow shelters after use, unless planning to re-use them in the near future. Also

backfill any large holes, particularly snow pits dug into skiable slopes.

## MOTOR VEHICLES

Four-wheelers, all-terrain-vehicles, dirt bikes, and snowmobiles offer fun and access to remote places for people who might otherwise be unable to enjoy the backcountry. But motor vehicles can also cause greater disturbance to the natural environment and to other people than just about any other form of backcountry recreation. Used carelessly or in the wrong place, motor vehicles cause erosion, disturb other people and wildlife, and damage plants. All the more reason to include their use under the leave-no-trace ethic.

- Before leaving home, check your vehicle for hitchhiking weeds.

- The easiest and best way for all motorized travelers to reduce damage to the backcountry is to stay on roads and trails. Do not ride off-trail.

- Ride only in areas open to motorized use, and stay on routes designated for your specific type of vehicle. When in doubt, ask the local land manager.

- Stay off wet or muddy roads, trails, and soils. Avoid streambanks, lakeshores, and wet meadows. Preserve motorized access by preventing erosion and other damage.

- Be considerate of other recreationists, especially hikers, stock users, skiers, paddlers, and other non-motorized

visitors. Keep noise to a minimum, especially around campsites.

- Cross streams at right angles and at slow speeds. Try to avoid stirring up silt and mud from the bottom, which can smother fish, spawning sites, and other aquatic life.

- Use mufflers and spark arresters. Noise is one of the main complaints given by other travelers when encountering motor vehicles in the backcountry. Spark arresters are required in most backcountry areas to reduce the risk of wildfire. During fire season, regulations may require you to carry a shovel, bucket, and other fire-fighting tools. Know and obey the regulations relevant to your particular mode of travel.

- Keep your vehicle in good working condition. Poorly running engines pollute more than those that are well-tuned and maintained. Inspect your machine before each ride to ensure that it's not leaking engine oil, coolant, transmission fluid, lubricant, or fuel. A spill in the backcountry can threaten the health of local plants, wildlife, and waterways. Also, tighten any loose parts to avoid leaving a trail of nuts and bolts.

- Keep a respectful distance from all wildlife. In general, studies indicate that motor vehicles cause less disturbance—or at least no greater disturbance—than people traveling under their own power. Researchers theorize that animals grow accustomed to the presence and noise of machines and do not perceive them as a threat unless approached too closely. When in doubt, back off. Never chase wildlife.

- Give all other trail users right-of-way. Stop and shut off your engine when meeting packstock on the trail.

- Wear helmets and other safety gear. Always ride in control. Land managers are more supportive of access for recreationists who take proper steps to minimize risks.

- Avoid skidding or spinning tires, especially on steep slopes or in muddy conditions.

### CLIMBING

Climbers face a number of challenges unique to their sport. Not surprisingly, they have developed some interesting solutions and protocols, some of which apply to leaving no trace.

- Many access and exit routes to popular climbs have webs of unofficial trails created by climbers. Try to halt the spread of such trails—keep foot traffic to a minimum and use existing trails whenever possible. Tread lightly when standing on belay—look for a rock or other durable surface to stand on and keep your pack, ropes, and other equipment off of fragile areas. After completing a climb, either rappel back down (if it's safe to do so), or choose a gradual, switchbacking route back to the bottom.

- Whenever possible, use removable protection (chocks or nuts, and cams). Permanent bolts mar the rock and take away the sense of discovery and challenge for subsequent climbers.

- Do your best to remove all ropes, slings, and other equipment from your route after the climb.

- Leave the rock face intact and as you found it.

- Avoid "gardening" (cleaning) cracks and on ledges.

- Climb as quietly as possible.

- Reduce or eliminate the use of chalk. If you must chalk up, use a natural-colored chalk that blends with the rock.

- Whenever possible, pack out all human waste. Use a poop tube on extended climbs.

- Pack out all trash, worn-out equipment, and excess food.

- Be courteous to other climbers. Always climb as though people were below—do not drop anything and strive to minimize rockfalls.

- Mountaineers should take into account the concerns listed under "Arctic and alpine tundra" and "Snow and ice" in the Special Environments chapter. Major peaks, such as Whitney, Denali, Rainier, Logan, and Robson, attract thousands of expeditions every year, making it all the more important to practice low-impact techniques.

## CAVING

Caves, especially deep ones, are essentially closed systems compared to habitats in the daylight world. Air exchange, temperature, humidity, and other factors are often fairly static. Natural features and processes are highly susceptible to damage. The main concern of the conscientious caver is to minimize change to the subterranean environment. Bring in as little as possible, leave nothing, and take nothing out.

- Leave natural features as you found them. Some surfaces, such as travertine, can be marred by a mere touch.
- Use temporary route markers. Trail a spool of twine on the way in, rewinding it on the way out. In dry caves or on longer routes, place reflective decals or tape along the route. Remove them on the way out.
- On brief cave trips, refrain from eating while in the cave. Any food, even dropped crumbs, can upset the cave's natural balance of nutrients and organisms.
- Leave the cave to defecate or urinate. If this is not possible, carry out all human waste.

## WATCHING WILDLIFE

Problems arise when we disturb wildlife, even when it happens unintentionally. Most animals are constantly engaged in an effort to survive—looking for food, eating, resting, watching for predators, mating, nesting, and rearing young. When humans interrupt, vital calories go uneaten, energy is wasted in fleeing the scene or blustering a defense, and sometimes young or weak animals are left exposed to harsh weather or predation.

The basic rule of thumb is: You are too close if the animal changes its behavior because of your presence (adapted from the American Birder's Association Code of Ethics).

- Always err on the side of caution—keep a respectful distance.
- Try to remain unseen, and find a vantage point downwind from the animal. Be quiet and minimize unnecessary movements.
- Use binoculars, a spotting scope, or a telephoto lens rather than moving closer.

## HUNTING AND FISHING

Hunting and fishing predate all other recreational pastimes, and the thrill of taking wild food continues to draw many people into the backcountry. What can hunters and anglers do to leave no trace? The first rule is to always ask first for permission to hunt or fish on private land.

## Guidelines for Fishing

- Know and obey the regulations.

- Keep only what you can eat; practice catch-and-release. Use barbless hooks. Land the fish quickly rather than playing it to exhaustion. To release a fish, cradle it in the water facing into the current (to help water flow over the gills) until the fish recovers and swims away.

- Lead sinkers, when ingested, are toxic to waterfowl and other wildlife. Use steel weights.

- Make an honest effort to recover all snagged flies, lures, and tangled line.

- Respect other anglers' territory.

- Follow local regulations for disposing of fish entrails. If a method is not specified, weigh the following options:

  –Pack entrails out in a plastic bag (not recommended in bear country).

  –Burn entrails in a hot fire. If any residue remains, pack it out in a plastic bag. (Only if burning food in fires is permitted and fire is appropriate.)

  –If local regulations permit it, and other options are not viable, pierce entrails, deflate, and toss them far out into deep water. Take care that entrails do not wash ashore near a likely campsite.

  –Bury entrails only as a last resort (and never in bear country), or when regulations require it.

- Wild and native trout are also at risk to whirling disease, a potentially fatal illness of trout and salmon. The tiny parasite that causes trout illness can survive within live fish, dead fish, and in water and riverbed mud.

---

**FOLLOW THESE DOs AND DON'Ts TO HELP PREVENT THE SPREAD OF WHIRLING DISEASE:**

1. Do remove all mud and aquatic plants from your vehicle, boat, anchor, trailer and axles, waders, boots, and fishing gear before departing the fishing access site or boat dock.

2. Do dry your boat equipment between river trips.

3. Don't transport fish from one body of water to another.

4. Don't dispose of fish entrails, skeletal parts, or other by-products in any body of water. (Note: you may be required to do this by local park service or forest service recommendations for disposal, but avoid it when practical.)

5. Don't collect or use minnows or sculpins for bait.

6. Don't use parts of trout, salmon, or whitefish for bait.

---

## Guidelines for Hunting

- Know and obey the regulations.
- Lead shot is toxic to wildlife; use steel shot.
- Take only clear, sure shots. Shoot only when certain of the target's identity.

- Know your weapon's range and verify a clear field of fire near and behind the target before shooting.
- Make every effort to track and dispatch a wounded animal.
- Follow local regulations for disposing of unused remains. In most areas, dressing the animal in the field is satisfactory. Make sure all parts of the carcass are far from any campsites, trails, or other sites likely to be used by people (this is especially important in bear country).

*Beyond Fair Chase* (Falcon 1994) by Jim Posewitz offers additional ethical guidelines for hunters.

# Special
# Environments

Most of the no-trace techniques described in this book can be used no matter where in the North American backcountry you travel. But in some special environments the standard techniques aren't always appropriate.

For example, when choosing a campsite on a remote river or lake, it's often best to disregard the standard 200-foot setback from water. Instead, pitch your tent on the beach or shore, below the high-water mark (when it is safe to do so). This way, trampling and other damage is confined to the sand or gravel shore, and any sign of your stay will be washed away by the next rise in water levels.

Sometimes special environments overlap. On a canoe trip through the Arctic, for instance, a campsite would encompass the river itself and its banks, tundra, and possibly snow and ice. It is important, then, to understand the no-trace techniques for each environment and to be able to choose wisely among them to minimize impacts.

All of the following suggestions are for traveling and camping in remote or pristine places. When visiting popular sites in special environments, follow the standard guidelines—concentrate use on existing trails and campsites.

## DESERTS

Deserts are defined by a scarcity of water and a poverty of soils. Recreational use here often concentrates around water sources in otherwise sparsely used areas. Minimizing impacts around such oases is crucial because most animals and plants are already stressed by temperature extremes, thirst, and hunger. Any added stress—such as trampling plants or spooking wildlife away from water or shade—reduces their margin for survival.

Desert plants and soils also grow and develop slowly, meaning they are also slow to recover from damage. Scars from a single incautious person will greet other visitors for years to come.

- Because use tends to concentrate around water sources, tread lightly around any surface water. Keep soap, human waste, and other pollutants out of dry washes, narrow canyons, potholes, and culverts that will carry runoff during rainstorms. Camp at least 400 yards from springs and other small water sources so that wildlife won't be discouraged from coming down to drink.

- Where water sources are small, take only enough water for drinking (treat or boil it first) and cooking. Removing larger amounts for washing or bathing can dramatically reduce water quality and deprive wildlife of a crucial drink.

- Use a cook stove and build no fires. Woody plants grow slowly here, and the supply of downed wood is too easily depleted.

- If possible, pack out all human waste. In the desert, a cat hole may prolong decomposition. For on-site disposal in areas with very little human use, it's better to scatter feces in small pieces on the open ground in an out-of-the-way spot. Sprinkle with sand to discourage flies. High heat and aridity will "cook" waste faster than it would decompose.

- Around camp, avoid urinating repeatedly in the same areas. Urine-saturated sand retains a strong odor and salt residues may attract unwanted animals.

- Use sand, slickrock, gravel washes, and other hard or barren surfaces for travel routes and campsites. Avoid areas of cryptobiotic crust—an extremely fragile "living soil."

*Cryptobiotic crust* is the foundation of life in the high desert. It provides a seedbed for the desert plant community and serves as a sponge, retaining the precious moisture of a dry climate. The crust is also the primary source for fixation of nitrogen, which is critical to all life in the desert. This crust is a complex community of microorganisms, the most important of which are called cyanobacteria.

When mature, cryptobiotic soil has a lumpy, black-tinged crust. In earlier stages, the crust is almost invisible. If you step on it, ride on it, or drive on it, it blows away and erodes, and then it takes many years, if not decades, to recover.

This is a prime reason to stay on trails and roads. If you have to hike off-trail, try to stay on slickrock or in canyon washes to prevent stepping on cryptobiotic crust.

## ARCTIC AND ALPINE TUNDRA

Compared to other environments, cold temperatures and a short growing season combine to give Arctic and alpine tundra the lowest ability to recover once damage has occurred. In one particularly fragile area, researchers in Colorado's Rocky Mountain National Park estimated that 70 to 100 years may pass before a high meadow would recover from just one season of off-trail foot traffic. In the far north, travelers sometimes stumble onto stone rings and circular depressions—evidence of native encampments from 1,000 years ago.

The Arctic and high alpine regions saw comparatively little human use for eons, but our technology and our drive to explore inhospitable places is rapidly ending that isolation. Even more so than in other environments, recreation in the Arctic and alpine regions places both the land and the people drawn to play in it at risk.

- Stay on established trails. If no trails exist, seek routes on bare mineral soil, rock, cobble streambeds, snow and ice, or other durable surfaces. Avoid stepping on moss, lichen, or succulents growing among rocks.

- Use a cookstove and build no fires. Leave what scant wood there is to return much-needed nutrients to the thin soil.

- Avoid travel during thaws or when soils are saturated with water. In the Arctic, summer trips are best made by boat. Winter travel by ski, snowshoe, or dogsled allows the widest choice of routes.

- Whenever possible, camp below the alpine zone—below timberline. When camping above timberline, confine all cooking, sleeping, and group activities to bedrock, talus, or snow.

- In the Arctic, camp on gravel bars or slumps of bare mineral soil. Limit your stay at any one site to two nights or less, and keep foot traffic to a minimum.

- Anticipate severe weather, which can cause delays and slow going. Pack extra food, fuel, and warm clothing to prevent the need for emergency campfires or camping in poor sites.

- Fecal bacteria can survive for years in alpine and Arctic tundra, even when buried properly in a cat hole. For this reason, never use a group latrine. Where human discovery is unlikely, smear waste on a rock or on the surface of the bare ground. Sun and weather will break it down faster than if it were buried.

- In the vast horizons of tundra regions, wildlife may not tolerate close approach. Keep at least a quarter mile away from all large animals.

## SNOW AND ICE

The advent of synthetic fabrics has dramatically increased cold-weather outdoor recreation, allowing more people to play on snow and ice. In particular, mountaineering on peaks such as Denali, Rainier, and Logan, and on Canada's ice-fields is no longer a sport limited to the wealthy or extremely hardy. And winter is no longer the "off" season.

Land managers are quickly catching up with this ava-lanche of recreation on snow and ice, but we can help minimize problems by modifying our leave-no-trace tech-niques to fit the winter environment.

- Avoid disturbing wildlife; know how to recognize and avoid winter feeding grounds and den sites.

- Pack out all garbage and all human waste.

- Strive to be inconspicuous to other people. Snow cover allows greater freedom of travel with little risk of trampling plants or soils. Take advantage of this by dispersing use—avoiding popular areas in favor of places few people go.

- Camp at least 400 yards from trails, other people, and obvious wildlife feeding or resting sites. Animals may be less accustomed to seeing people during winter, so give them more room.

- Dismantle all snow structures and backfill large holes when breaking camp, unless you plan to use them again in the near future.

## COASTS, RIVERS, AND LAKES

When traveling along a coast, river, or lakeshore, we tend to watch the water—waves, whitewater, or a mirror-calm surface. But from a no-trace perspective, the adjacent landscape—the terrain, climate, and habitat type—must also remain in focus.

- Take into account times of high and low water when planning your trip. Know how different water levels will affect your route and campsite options.

- Confine camping and other activities to the beach or shore, below the high-water mark or monthly high-tide line (when it is safe to do so). Any sign of your stay will be washed away by the next ebb and flow in water levels.

- The plants and soils in the zone just above the high-water mark can be highly sensitive to trampling and other damage. When traveling away from the beach or shore, go well inland to avoid this fragile zone.

- Keep a respectful distance from marine and aquatic animals. Stay at least 200 yards from off-shore rocks, sea stacks, and kelp beds.

- Use caution around coral reefs, which can be seriously damaged by boat hulls, propellers, and even human touch.

- Build campfires only as needed and only where downed wood is abundant. Build the fire directly on the surface of the sand or gravel shore below the daily high-tide line or below the annual high-water mark. Use small pieces of wood and burn them down to ash.

- In truly remote, unpopulated coastal areas, deposit feces on the beach well below the daily high-tide line. Wave action and marine bacteria will make quick work of it. On rivers, lakes, and along more populated coasts, pack out all human waste. Never bury waste in sand.

- Keep all other waste and garbage out of the water.

## WETLANDS

- Plan your trip to avoid disturbing wildlife, especially migrating or nesting waterfowl.

- Inspect clothes and equipment, including boat hulls, for hitch-hiking weeds, algae, and other organisms, such as zebra mussels. Dump water out of boats before traveling to another area to prevent the spread of unwanted organisms and plants.

- Camp on sand or gravel beaches where available. When traveling by boat, consider sleeping in it.

- In the South, many wetland areas provide chickees—wooden platforms on stilts—for camping. Use a free-standing tent (stakes and nails are prohibited).

- Use a stove for cooking and punk sticks rather than a campfire to smoke out mosquitoes.

- Keep all waste and contaminants out of the water. Pack out all human waste.

# Trail's End

When you come back home from your next backcountry trip, think for a moment about any traces of your visit you may have left behind. A faint trail of footprints? A deer or coyote sniffing at your scent where you paused for lunch along the trail?

If you follow the guidelines in this book, these may be the only outward signs of your passage. But you may also discover a more telling inward sign. Most people are surprised by how rewarding—how good—it feels to successfully leave no trace.

A large part of this inner reward is the knowledge that you can leave a place unspoiled for your next visit or the next person to come along, or even for the next generation. Practicing no-trace techniques ensures that we will all continue to find opportunities to have fun and seek renewal in wild, pristine places.

The other part of the reward is that no-trace camping itself can be less work and more fun than the old routines. Skeptical? Consider making a trial run—a low-mileage overnighter or day trip. Wait for good weather and pick a familiar destination. Then go light and try out the techniques in this book. Go without a campfire. Use leaves instead of toilet paper. Wear a pair of comfortable running shoes instead of the old boots. Plan a no-cook menu and leave the cookstove at home. But be careful—a lighter pack, fewer chores around camp, a sense of satisfaction upon leaving a clean camp . . . this could be habit forming!

Finally, share your new knowledge and skills with people you meet on the trails. Set a good example by keeping a clean camp, staying on the trail, and protecting lakes, rivers, and streams. Many people have heard about the no-trace ethic, but they may not know how to reduce their impact when setting up camp, building a fire, or disposing of waste. Offer to lend a hand and explain why no-trace techniques work and why they're important. Kids are especially open to the ideas in this book. Share your enthusiasm! Remember, too, that not everyone understands the need for the no-trace approach; don't try to force the issue if someone is resistant or argumentative. It's far better to teach by example.

If you want to get more formal training in leave-no-trace techniques, or for educational materials for your local outdoor club or schools, contact one of the organizations listed in the Appendix.

| **TECHNIQUES SUMMARY** |
| --- |
| Plan ahead, prepare well, prevent problems before they occur. |
| Know and obey local regulations. |
| Walk softly—wear shoes with shallow tread. |
| Check your clothing and gear for noxious weeds. |
| Stay on trails. Walk single file. |
| Where there are no trails, travel on durable surfaces or spread out. |
| Leave all cultural artifacts undisturbed. |
| Keep noise to a minimum. |
| Keep a clean kitchen and camp. |
| Build no fires. |
| Keep contaminants away from streams and lakes. |
| Pack out all garbage and waste. |
| Keep a respectful distance from all wildlife. |

## Organizations

**American Hiking Society**
1422 Fenwick Lane
Silver Spring, MD 20910
888-766-HIKE, ext. 1
www.americanhiking.org

**Leave No Trace, Inc.**
P.O. Box 997
Boulder, CO 80306
(800) 332-4100
www.lnt.org

**National Parks and Conservation Association**
1015 31st Street N.W.
Washington, D.C. 20007
(202) 944-8530

**Tread Lightly!**
298 24th Street
Suite 325-C
Ogden, UT 84401
(801) 627-0077

## Suggested Reading

**Bear Aware**
by Bill Schneider.
Falcon® Publishing, Inc.
ISBN 1-56044-456-8

**How To Shit in the Woods**
by Kathleen Meyer
Ten Speed Press
ISBN 0-89815-319-0

**Soft Paths**
by Bruce Hampton
and David Cole
Stackpole Books
ISBN 0-8117-2234-1

**Walking Softly in the Wilderness**
by John Hart
Sierra Club Books
ISBN 0-87156-813-6

**Wildland Recreation**
by William E. Hammitt and
David N. Cole
John Wiley & Sons, Inc.
ISBN 0-47187-291-1

**Treading Lightly with Pack Animals: A Guide to Low Impact Travel in the Backcountry**
by Dan Aadland
Mountain Press
ISBN 0-87842-297-8

**Wild Country Companion: The Ultimate Guide to No-trace Outdoor Recreation and Wilderness Safety**
by Will Harmon
Falcon® Publishing Co., Inc
ISBN 1-56044-169-0

## THE AUTHOR

An enthusiastic backcountry wanderer, Will Harmon lives in Helena, Montana, with his wife Rose and their two sons, Evan and Ben. His many years of wilderness experience include several seasons working as a guide and USDA Forest Service wilderness ranger. He is the author of *Wild Country Companion: The Ultimate Guide to No-trace Outdoor Recreation and Wilderness Safety, Hiking Alberta,* and *Mountain Biking Bozeman,* and he is currently working on several more titles.

**FALCON**GUIDES ® Leading the Way™

## WILDERNESS SURVIVAL
*by Suzanne Swedo*

This pocket-sized guide contains helpful information on trip planning, staying found, what to do if you get lost, and survival priorities.

## BEAR AWARE
*by Bill Schneider*

Hiking in bear country can be very safe if hikers follow the guidelines summarized in this small, "packable" book. Extensively reviewed by bear experts, the book contains the latest information on the intriguing science of bear-human interactions. *Bear Aware* can not only make your hike safer, but it can help you avoid the fear of bears that can take the edge off your trip.

## MOUNTAIN LION ALERT
*By Steve Torres*

Recent mountain lion attacks have received national attention. Although infrequent, these and other lion attacks raise concern for public safety. *Mountain Lion Alert* contains helpful advice for mountain bikers, trail runners, horse riders, pet owners, and suburban landowners on how to reduce the chances of mountain lion-human conflicts.

**Also Available:**

*Avalanche Aware, Backpacking Tips, Climbing Safely, Desert Hiking Tips, Hiking with Dogs, Hiking with Kids, Reading Weather, Route Finding, Using GPS, Wild Country Companion, Wilderness First Aid, Wilderness Survival,*

*To order these titles check with your local bookseller or call FALCON® at 1-800-582-2665.*

www.Falcon.com

## Hiking

Best Hikes Along the Continental
    Divide
Hiking Alaska
Hiking Arizona
Hiking Arizona's Cactus Country
Hiking the Beartooths
Hiking Big Bend National Park
Hiking the BobMarshall Country
Hiking California
Hiking California's Desert Parks
Hiking Carlsbad/Guadalupe
Hiking Colorado
Hiking Colorado, Vol.II
Hiking Colorado's Summits
Hiking Colorado's Weminuche
    Wilderness
Hiking the ColumbiaRiver Gorge
Hiking Florida
Hiking Georgia
Hiking Glacier/Waterton Lakes
Hiking Grand Canyon
Hiking Grand Staircase-Escalante
Hiking Grand TetonNational Park
Hiking Great Basin Nat'l Park
Hiking Hot Springs in the Pacific
    Northwest
Hiking Idaho
Hiking Maine
Hiking Maryland and Delaware
Hiking Michigan
Hiking Minnesota
Hiking Montana
Hiking Mount RainierNational Park
Hiking Mount St. Helens
Hiking Nevada
Hiking New Hampshire
Hiking New Mexico
Hiking New Mexico's Gila Wilderness
Hiking New York

Hiking North Carolina
Hiking the North Cascades
Hiking Northern Arizona
Hiking Northern California
Hiking Olympic National Park
Hiking Oregon
Hiking Oregon's Central Cascades
Hiking Oregon's Eagle Cap
Hiking Oregon's Mt. Hood
Hiking Oregon's Three Sisters
Hiking Pennsylvania
Hiking Ruins Seldom Seen
Hiking Shenandoah
Hiking the Sierra Nevada
Hiking South Carolina
Hiking South Dakota's BlackHills
    Country
Hiking Southern New England
Hiking Tennessee
Hiking Texas
Hiking Utah
Hiking Utah's Summits
Hiking Vermont
Hiking Virginia
Hiking Washington
Hiking Wyoming
Hiking Wyoming's CloudPeak
    Wilderness
Hiking Wyoming's Teton
    andWashakie Wilderness
Hiking Wyoming's WindRiver
    Range
Hiking YellowstoneNational Park
Hiking Yosemite
Hiking Zion & Bryce Canyon
Exploring Canyonlands & Arches
Wild Country Companion
Wild Montana
Wild Utah

# FALCON GUIDES® Leading the Way™

Published in cooperation with Defenders of Wildlife, the Watchable Wildlife® Series is the official series of guidebooks for the National Watchable Wildlife Program. This highly successful program is a unique partnership of state and federal agencies and a private organization. Each full-color guidebook in the Watchable Wildlife® series features detailed site descriptions, side trips, viewing tips, and easy-to-follow maps.

## WILDLIFE VIEWING GUIDES

Alaska Wildlife Viewing Guide
Arizona Wildlife Viewing Guide
California Wildlife Viewing Guide
Colorado Wildlife Viewing Guide
Florida Wildlife Viewing Guide
Indiana Wildlife Vewing Guide
Iowa Wildlife Viewing Guide
Kentucky Wildlife Viewing Guide
Massachusetts Wildlife Viewing Guide
Montana Wildlife Viewing Guide
Nebraska Wildlife Viewing Guide
Nevada Wildlife Viewing Guide
New Hampshire Wildlife Viewing Guide
New Jersey Wildlife Viewing Guide
New Mexico Wildlife Viewing Guide

New York Wildlife Viewing Guide
North Carolina Wildlife Viewing Guide
North Dakota Wildlife Viewing Guide
Ohio Wildlife Viewing Guide
Oregon Wildlife Viewing Guide
Puerto Rico & the Virgin Islands Wildlife Viewing Guide
Tennessee Wildlife Viewing Guide
Texas Wildlife Viewing Guide
Utah Wildlife Viewing Guide
Vermont Wildlife Viewing Guide
Virginia Wildlife Viewing Guide
Washington Wildlife Viewing Guide
West Virginia Wildife Viewing Guide
Wisconsin Wildlife Viewing Guide

*To order any of these books, check with your
local bookseller or call Falcon® at
1-800-582-2665.*
www.Falcon.com